Mercury

ELAINE LANDAU

Children's Press®
A Division of Scholastic Inc.
New York Toronto London Auckland Sydney
Mexico City New Delhi Hong Kong
Danbury, Connecticut

Content Consultant

Michelle Yehling

Astronomy Education Consultant

Aurora, Illinois

Reading Consultant

Cecilia Minden-Cupp, PhD

Early Literacy Consultant and Author

Library of Congress Cataloging-in-Publication Data

Landau, Elaine.
 Mercury / by Elaine Landau.
    p. cm.—(A true book)
 Includes bibliographical references and index.
 ISBN-13: 978-0-531-12561-8 (lib. bdg.)   978-0-531-14791-7 (pbk.)
 ISBN-10: 0-531-12561-0 (lib. bdg.)   0-531-14791-6 (pbk.)
 1. Mercury (Planet)—Juvenile literature. I. Title. II. Series.
 QB611.L36 2007
 523.41—dc22   2007012277

All rights reserved. Published in 2008 by Children's Press, an imprint of Scholastic Inc. Published simultaneously in Canada. Printed in the United States of America.
SCHOLASTIC, CHILDREN'S PRESS, A TRUE BOOK, and associated logos are trademarks and/or registered trademarks of Scholastic Inc.
1 2 3 4 5 6 7 8 9 10 R 17 16 15 14 13 12 11 10 09

Find the Truth!

Everything you are about to read is true *except* for one of the sentences on this page.

Which one is **TRUE**?

T or F The ancient Greeks thought that Mercury was two different planets.

T or F Mercury is very cold at night even though it is so close to the sun.

Find the answer in this book.

3

Contents

THE **BIG** TRUTH!

Mercury's Mystery

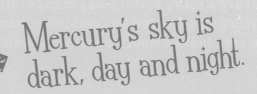

Mercury's sky is dark, day and night.

Mercury's rocky surface has many craters and cliffs. This image of Mercury was created by combining many separate images of the planet. One area looks smooth because scientists have no images of that part.

CHAPTER 1

A Trip to Mercury

It would take a spaceship about six months to travel directly to Mercury.

How much do you already know about Mercury? You might know that Mercury is the planet closest to the sun. You might also know that it is a very small planet. But there is much more to learn about Mercury. Let's take a trip there and have a closer look.

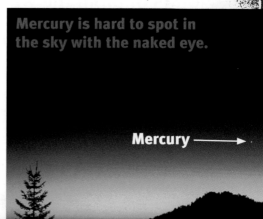

Mercury is hard to spot in the sky with the naked eye.

Mercury ⟶

7

This illustration shows Earth's moon peeking out from the planet's atmosphere.

Your trip would begin in a spaceship on Earth. Powerful rockets would blast you into the air. You would pass through Earth's **atmosphere**. An atmosphere is a blanket of gases that surrounds a planet or a moon. You would have a great view once you got above the atmosphere. There would be no clouds or air in the way. The black sky would be filled with thousands of bright stars.

Mercury is only slightly larger than Earth's moon.

As you flew further toward Mercury, Earth would seem to get smaller. The sun would begin to look bigger. You might fly past Venus. As you got closer to Mercury, you would begin to see the planet's rough surface. Mercury is full of holes and cliffs.

The surfaces of Earth's moon and Mercury look alike. Scientists believe the planet's outer layer may be made up of materials similar to those on the moon.

Earth's moon

Mercury

You could probably find a good spot to land on Mercury's rocky surface. However, you might not want to leave your air-conditioned spaceship. Mercury is the closest planet to the sun. That makes it extremely hot during the day.

You would need a space suit with its own air tank if you wanted to explore the planet. There is no air to breathe on Mercury. The space suit would also have to protect you from Mercury's extreme heat. It would have to protect you from the cold as well. Mercury really cools down at night!

From Mercury, the sun would look about three times bigger than it does from Earth.

Without the protection of a space suit, a human being would survive for little more than one minute in space.

Mercury

This is a photograph of Mercury passing in front of the sun. It was taken with a special telescope that blocks out the sun's dangerous rays.

CHAPTER 2

Mercury in the Solar System

Mercury travels faster around the sun than any other planet.

To get to Mercury on a spaceship, you would fly through part of the **solar system**. The solar system contains the sun and all the objects that travel around it. To find your way to Mercury, you would need to steer your spaceship toward the sun. Turn the page for a look at the solar system from above.

Mercury's Solar System

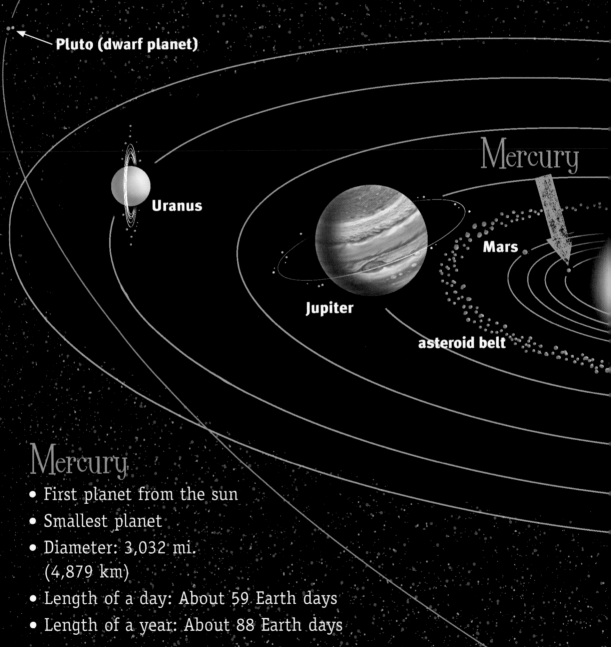

Pluto (dwarf planet)

Uranus

Mercury

Jupiter

Mars

asteroid belt

Mercury

- First planet from the sun
- Smallest planet
- Diameter: 3,032 mi.
  (4,879 km)
- Length of a day: About 59 Earth days
- Length of a year: About 88 Earth days

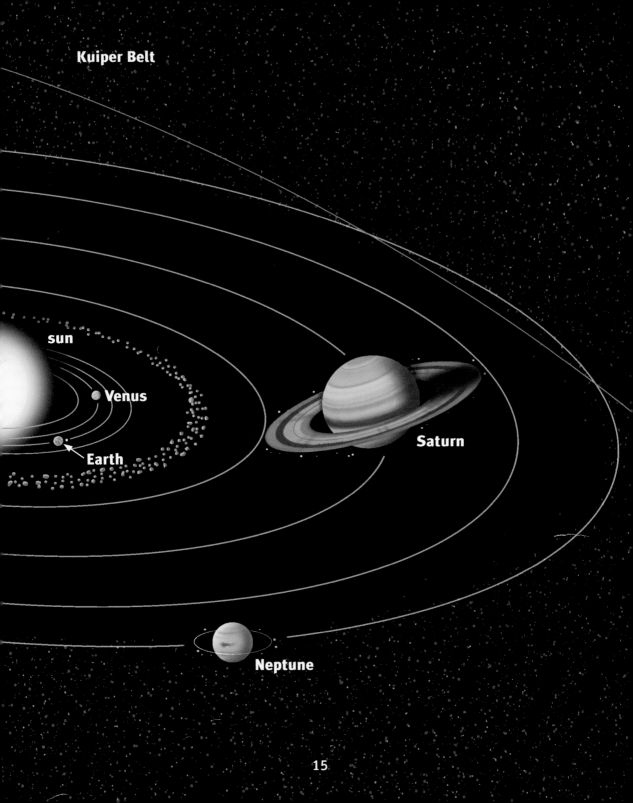

The Hale-Bopp comet was discovered in the mid-1990s. It is one of the brightest comets ever studied.

Comets sometimes fall into the sun and burn up.

There are eight planets in the solar system. The planets are Mercury, Venus, Earth, Mars, Jupiter, Saturn, Uranus, and Neptune.

The solar system also has other objects, such as three known **dwarf planets** and at least 162 moons. There are also **asteroids** and **comets**. Asteroids are large chunks of rock that speed through space. Comets are big lumps of ice and rock that travel around the sun.

Mercury on the Move

The sun is at the center of the solar system. The planets **orbit**, or travel around, the sun. Planets orbit in a flattened circle called an ellipse (ee-LIPS). Mercury is closer to the sun than Earth is, so Mercury's orbit is smaller than Earth's.

The time it takes a planet to orbit the sun once equals one year on that planet. Mercury is speedy. It moves through space at about 110,000 miles (180,000 kilometers) per hour. And Mercury is close to the sun, so its orbit is small. Mercury needs only about 88 Earth days to orbit the sun once.

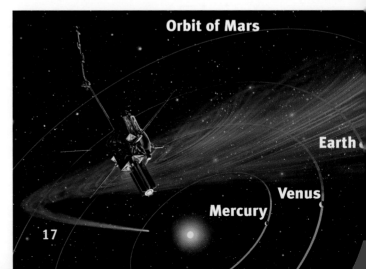

This illustration shows a spacecraft collecting information about the solar system. The purple lines show the orbits of the inner planets.

Orbit of Mars

Earth

Venus

Mercury

How Mercury Got Its Name

Mercury is sometimes visible in the morning in the east. At other times, you can see it in the evening, in the west. People once thought they were seeing two different planets. But scientists in ancient Greece realized that Mercury was one planet that seemed to race across the sky.

The name Mercury was taken from the Roman messenger god. Messengers deliver things. Mercury had wings on his helmet and sandals. He was very fast, just like the planet that was named after him.

Here Mercury is shown with a wing on his head. The wing is a symbol of his speed. The Greeks called him Hermes.

18

A Day on Mercury

Mercury spins on its **axis** while it orbits the sun. An axis is an imaginary line that runs from north to south through the center of a planet or a moon.

The time it takes a planet to **rotate** once on its axis equals one day on that planet. It takes Mercury about 59 Earth days to rotate on its axis. This means that a day on Mercury is about 59 Earth days long. So Mercury has very long days and very short years.

One day on Mercury is more than half as long as a year on the planet!

The red arrow in this diagram shows the direction of Mercury's rotation. As the planet rotates, new parts move into the sunlight.

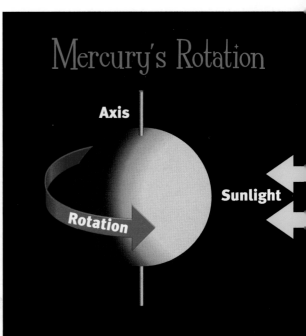

Mercury's Rotation

Axis

Sunlight

Rotation

Size and Gravity

Mercury is the smallest planet in our solar system. It is even smaller than some moons in the solar system. Mercury's size affects the planet's **gravity.**

Gravity is the force that pulls objects toward each other. Earth's gravity makes you come back down after you jump into the air. Some objects have more gravity than other objects.

If you weighed 100 pounds on Earth, you would weigh only 38 pounds on Mercury!

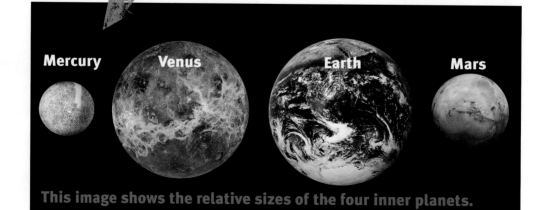

Mercury   Venus   Earth   Mars

This image shows the relative sizes of the four inner planets.

Gravity is based on an object's **mass**, or the amount of stuff in an object. Mercury's mass is less than Earth's mass, so Mercury has less gravity.

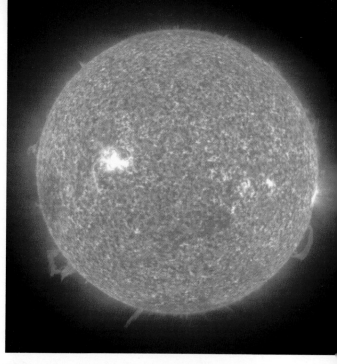

The sun contains more than 99 percent of the mass in the solar system.

If you traveled to Mercury, you would weigh less than you do on Earth. You would feel lighter. You could jump higher than you can on Earth.

The massive sun has a huge amount of gravity. The sun's gravity tugs on Mercury and all the other planets in the solar system. That gravity keeps the planets orbiting the sun rather than flying off into space!

This is an illustration of Mercury with Earth and Venus in the background.

Venus

Earth

CHAPTER 3

Always Hot? No, It's Not!

If you were standing on Mercury, Earth would look like a bright blue star in the sky.

You might find blazing-hot temperatures if you landed on Mercury. It can get as hot as 840°F (450°C)! This makes sense for a planet close to the sun. Mercury is not always hot, however. If you landed on it at night, you would be frozen solid. There may even be ice on Mercury. How is that possible?

Mercury's surface is extremely hot during the day. At night, temperatures can drop as low as −279°F (−173°C). How can a hot planet get so cold?

Mercury and Earth both have atmospheres, but the two atmospheres are very different. Earth has a thick atmosphere. It soaks up heat from the sun all day. At night, the atmosphere holds on to some of this heat. It is like a warm blanket around Earth. So Earth does not get too cold.

This drawing shows the clouds in Earth's atmosphere from space. Earth's moon is in the background.

Earth's atmosphere is more than a billion times thicker than Mercury's.

In this illustration of Mercury from space, it is daytime on the right side and night on the left.

Mercury has a very thin atmosphere. It is so thin that it is hard to tell where the atmosphere ends and empty space begins.

Sun bakes the sunny side of Mercury. The thin atmosphere can't hold on to this heat, however. Heat escapes from the dark half of the planet. This half gets freezing cold! The difference between daytime and nighttime temperatures on Mercury can be as much as 1,000°F (600°C).

Mercury has craters of all shapes and sizes. Some are deep and dark. Scientists think that ice may lie in deep, dark craters near Mercury's north and south poles.

Shaded craters such as these may hold ice.

Brahms crater is about 50 miles (75 km) in diameter

Mercury's Mystery

How Could Ice Survive Mercury's Heat?

Telescopes on Earth may have found evidence of ice on Mercury. But how could ice survive Mercury's long, blazing-hot days? Scientists don't know—but they do have an idea. Some of Mercury's craters are so deep that sunlight never reaches the bottom. Maybe the ice doesn't melt because it stays in the shade.

Mercury has areas that are full of craters, and other areas that are smooth planes. The planet has some craters called ray craters, where light-colored material was blasted out as the crater was formed.

ray crater

CHAPTER 4

What Is Mercury Made Of?

If Earth were the size of a baseball, Mercury would be the size of a golf ball.

Mercury seems to be a lot different from Earth. Still, the two planets are alike in some ways. How is Mercury like your planet? Read on to find out.

The Surface of Mercury

Like Earth, Mercury is a terrestrial (tuh-RES-tree-uhl) planet. Terrestrial planets have a solid surface made of rocks. Mars and Venus are the other terrestrial planets in our solar system.

The rest of the planets in our solar system are called gas giants. They are huge planets made mostly of gas and liquid.

If you tried to stand on a gas giant such as Jupiter, you would sink into the planet.

Jupiter is the largest planet in our solar system.

Inside Mercury

If you dug a hole to the center of Mercury, what do you think you might find? **Astronomers** do not know exactly what the inside of Mercury is like. However, they think it might have layers similar to Earth's layers.

The surfaces of both Mercury and Earth are made up of a hard, thin crust. Below the crust is a layer of hot, soft rock. In the center of the planet is a solid part called the core.

How do astronomers know what's inside other planets? Instruments on spacecraft gather information about a planet. Astronomers use this information to understand what the planet is made of. Their ideas may change as they learn more about Mercury.

Craters on the Surface

Just like Earth's moon, Mercury has many craters. Craters are large holes that are created when space rocks and other objects crash into a planet.

The largest crater on Mercury is called the Caloris Basin. The Caloris Basin is about 808 miles (1,300 km) wide. This crater is even wider than the state of Texas. Astronomers think a giant asteroid may have crashed into the planet.

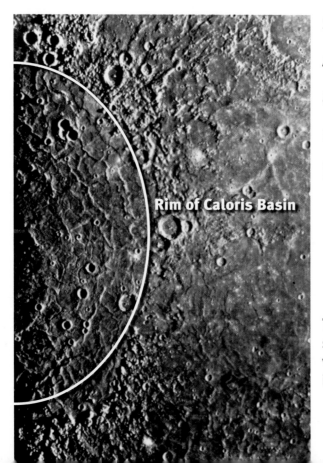

Rim of Caloris Basin

The Caloris Basin is surrounded by a ring of very tall mountains. Its interior is full of ridges.

Mercury and Venus are the only planets without moons.

This photo shows Venus's surface. Venus is the only planet in the solar system that is named after a goddess, not a god.

Mercury has many long cliffs on its surface. Some of these cliffs are 1 mile (1.6 km) high. Mercury has more cliffs than any other planet or moon in our solar system.

Earth has one big thing that Mercury does not have, though. Earth has one moon. Some planets have lots of moons, but Mercury has no moons at all.

This illustration shows a view of the sun from Mercury.

CHAPTER 5

Missions to Mercury

If you went to Mercury, you would see two sunrises and two sunsets each day.

Astronomers want to know more about Mercury. Until recently, there had only been one mission to that planet. Find out what scientists learned from that mission—and what they hope the latest mission will uncover.

This photo shows scientists building *Mariner 10* in 1973.

The *Mariner 10* Mission

Mariner 10 was a space probe, or a spacecraft that does not have astronauts on board. *Mariner 10* was launched toward Mercury on November 3, 1973. Much of what we know about Mercury came from that mission.

Mariner 10 did not fly directly to Mercury. Instead, it headed toward Venus. It got close enough to be pulled by Venus's gravity. That gravity gave *Mariner 10* a boost. Like a slingshot, Venus's gravity flung the spacecraft toward Mercury. *Mariner 10* was the first spacecraft to use gravity in this way.

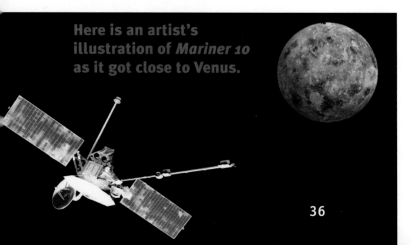

Here is an artist's illustration of *Mariner 10* as it got close to Venus.

Mariner 10 photographed almost half of Mercury's surface.

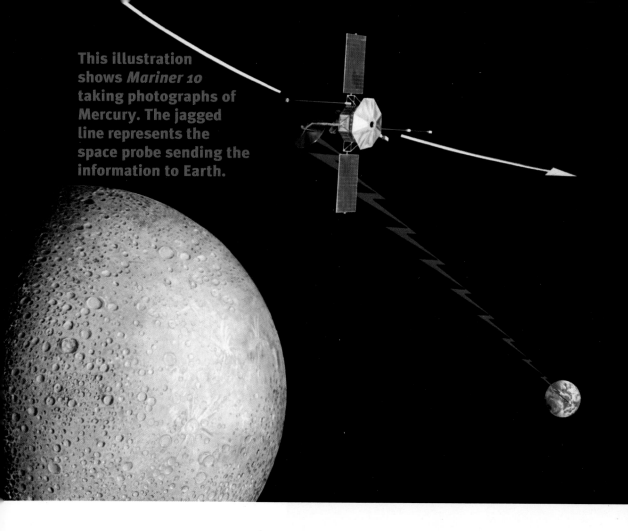

This illustration shows *Mariner 10* taking photographs of Mercury. The jagged line represents the space probe sending the information to Earth.

Mariner 10 flew by Mercury three times in 1974 and 1975. Instruments on the spacecraft gathered information about the craters, cliffs, and other features on Mercury's surface. They also measured Mercury's temperatures and studied its atmosphere.

The *MESSENGER* Mission

Astronomers were excited by what they learned from *Mariner 10*'s mission. But there was still a lot more to learn about Mercury. So *MESSENGER* was launched on August 3, 2004.

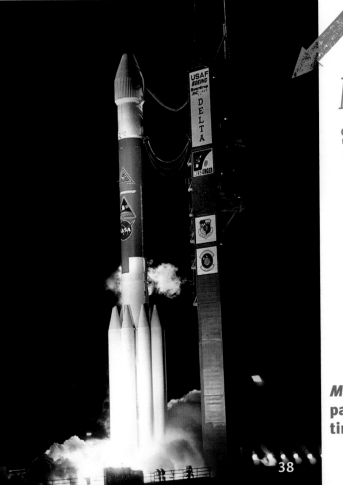

MESSENGER stands for MErcury Surface, Space ENvironment, GEchemistry, and Ranging.

MESSENGER is expected to pass Mercury for the first time in 2008.

Protecting the
MESSENGER

Mercury is close to the sun. Up close, the sun's strong rays could melt a space probe. *MESSENGER* was going to need special protection.

When *MESSENGER* reaches Mercury, it will photograph areas of the planet that *Mariner 10* didn't.

Have you ever seen a sunshade in the front windshield of a car? Scientists designed a high-tech sunshade for *MESSENGER*. Sunshades reflect, or bounce back, the sun's strong rays. *MESSENGER'S* sunshade will keep the probe from getting too hot.

The sun's rays aren't always bad. **Solar panels** on the probe collect the sun's energy. This energy can power *MESSENGER* on its long journey.

MESSENGER is going on a long trip. It already flew past Earth once. It flew past Venus twice. *MESSENGER* got a boost from Venus like *Mariner 10* did. It used Venus's gravity to gain speed and change direction.

Next, *MESSENGER* will fly past Mercury three times. On March 18, 2011, it should begin to orbit Mercury. The plan is for *MESSENGER* to orbit Mercury and gather information for one year.

Missions to Mercury Timeline

1973
On November 3, *Mariner 10* is launched from

1974
Mariner 10 reaches Mercury. It flies past the planet and takes

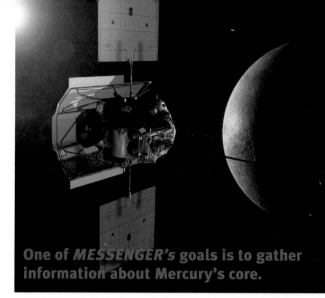

One of *MESSENGER's* goals is to gather information about Mercury's core.

MESSENGER will send back the first complete set of pictures of the entire planet. It will collect information about the materials that make up Mercury. *MESSENGER* will help astronomers learn more about the gases surrounding Mercury. It will also study the craters where ice may be located.

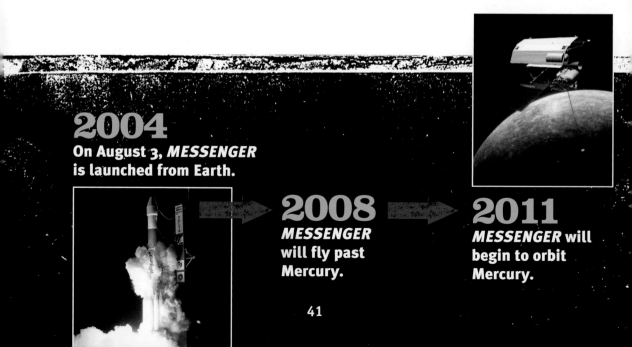

2004
On August 3, *MESSENGER* is launched from Earth.

2008
MESSENGER will fly past Mercury.

2011
MESSENGER will begin to orbit Mercury.

There is still a lot more to know about Mercury. *MESSENGER* and future missions might solve the mystery of Mercury's ice. They might tell scientists more about what Mercury and its atmosphere are made of. These missions will give us a better idea of what it would be like to visit the little, fast-moving planet next to the sun. ★

Astronomers have spent years trying to improve space probes so that they will be able to withstand the incredible heat of the sun as they study Mercury.

True Statistics

Classification: Terrestrial planet

Named after: Roman messenger god

Diameter: 3,032 mi. (4,879 km)

Number of moons: 0

Surface temperature: Between −279°F (−173°C) and 801°F (427°C)

Distance from the sun: About 36 million mi. (58 million km)

100-pound (45 kg) person would weigh: 38 lb. (17 kg)

Length of a day: About 59 Earth days

Length of a year: About 88 Earth days

First mission: *Mariner 10*, 1973

Number of times *Mariner 10* flew past Mercury: 3

Name of current mission: *MESSENGER*

Did you find the truth?

F The ancient Greeks thought that Mercury was two different planets.

T Mercury is very cold at night even though it is so close to the sun.

43

Resources

Books

Cole, Michael D. *Mercury: The First Planet*. Berkeley Heights, NJ: Enslow Publishers, 2001.

Lassieur, Allison. *Astronauts*. Danbury, CT: Children's Press, 2000.

O'Connell, Kim A. *Mercury*. Berkeley Heights, NJ: Myreportlinks.com Books, 2005.

Orr, Tamra. *The Telescope*. Danbury, CT: Franklin Watts, 2004.

Stille, Darlene R. *Mercury*. Mankato, MN: The Child's World, 2003.

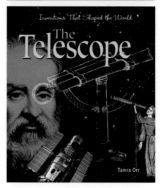

Organizations and Web Sites

Astronomy for Kids—Mercury
www.kidsastronomy.com/mercury.htm
Visit this site for more information and pictures of Mercury.

NASA: The Space Place
spaceplace.jpl.nasa.gov
Visit this site for an enjoyable lesson on space.

National Space Society
www.nss.org
1620 I Street NW, Suite 615
Washington, DC 20006
202-429-1600
This organization is committed to helping humans live and work in space.

Places to Visit

Kennedy Space Center
John F. Kennedy
Space Center
Kennedy Space Center,
Florida 32899
www.ksc.nasa.gov
Take a tour of KSC's giant rockets and launch pads.

Smithsonian National Air and Space Museum
Independence Avenue at 4th Street, SW
Washington, DC 20560
202-633-1000
www.nasm.si.edu
See the world's largest collection of historic airplanes and spaceships.

Important Words

asteroids (AS-tuh-roidz) – large pieces of rock that orbit the sun

astronomers (uh-STRAW-nuh-murz) – scientists who study the planets, stars, and space

atmosphere (AT-mu-sfihr) – the blanket of gases that surrounds a planet or other object

axis (AK-siss) – an imaginary line that runs through the center of a planet or other object

comets – large chunks of rock and ice that travel around the sun

dwarf planets – bodies in the solar system that orbit the sun, have a constant (nearly round) shape, are not moons, and have orbits that overlap with the orbits of other bodies

gravity – a force that pulls two objects together

mass – the amount of matter, or stuff, in an object

orbit – to travel around an object such as a sun or planet

rotate – to spin on an axis

solar panels – metal sheets designed to collect the sun's energy and turn it into electricity

solar system (SOH-lur SISS-tuhm) – a sun and all the objects that travel around it

Index

About the Author

Award-winning author Elaine Landau has a bachelor's degree from New York University and a master's degree in library and information science from Pratt Institute.

She has written more than 300 non-fiction books for children and young adults. Although Ms. Landau often writes on science topics, she especially likes writing about planets and space.

She lives in Miami, Florida, with her husband and son. The trio can often be spotted at the Miami Museum of Science and Space Transit Planetarium. You can visit Elaine Landau at her Web site: www.elainelandau.com.

PHOTOGRAPHS © 2008: Alamy Images/Pictor International/ImageState: 24; Art Resource, NY/Erich Lessing/Kunsthistorisches Museum, Vienna, Austria: 18; Corbis Images/Roger Ressmeyer: 33 (NASA), 11; European Space Agency/Hinode JAXA/NASA/PPARC: 12; Getty Images: 37 (MPI), cover, 3, 4 bottom, 27 (William Radcliffe), 16 (Roger Ressmeyer), 35 (Time Life Pictures); NASA: back cover, 5 bottom, 39, 41 top, 41 bottom right (JHU/APL), 30, 36, 42 (JPL), 9 right (JPL/Northwestern University), 9 left, 20 (Lunar and Planetary Institute), 21 (SOHO), 4 top, 26, 38, 40 left, 41 bottom left; Pat Rasch: 19 (NASA), 14, 15; Photo Researchers, NY: 22 (Chris Butler), 5 top, 34 (David A. Hardy), 17 (David R. Hardy/Courtesy PPARC), 25 (Roger Harris), 32, 40 right (NASA), 8 (SPL), 6 (USGS), 28 (Detlev van Ravenswaay), 7 (Frank Zullo); Photodisc, Inc.: 29; Scholastic Library Publishing, Inc.: 44.